Seymour Simon

SUPER STORMS

SEASTAR BOOKS · NEW YORK

This book is dedicated to my grandson Jeremy.

Title page photograph: A lightning bolt struck this tree, causing it to explode into a thousand splinters.

Special thanks to reading consultant Dr. Linda B. Gambrell, Director of the School of Education at Clemson University, past president of the National Reading Conference, and past board member of the International Reading Association.

Permission to use the following photographs is gratefully acknowledged:
Front cover: © Keith Kent/SPL, Photo Researchers, Inc.; title page: © J.H. Robinson, Photo Researchers, Inc.; pages 2–3: © Ray Ellis, Photo Researchers, Inc.; pages 4–5: U.S. Government Commerce National Severe Storms Laboratory/NGS Image Collection; pages 6–7: © George Post/Science Photo Library, Photo Researchers, Inc.; pages 8–9: © Kent Wood/Science Source, Photo Researchers, Inc.; pages 10–11: © Kul Bhatia, Photo Researchers, Inc.; pages 12–13: NOAA Photo Library, NOAA Central Library, OAR/ERL/National Severe Storms Laboratory (NSSL); page 12 insert, 32: Howard Bluestein, Photo Researchers, Inc.; pages 14–15: © Nancie Battaglia; pages 16–17: © Science VU/Visuals Unlimited; pages 18–19: © AFP/Corbis; pages 22–23: NOAA, NESDIS, Science Source, Photo Researchers, Inc.; pages 24–25: © Annie Griffiths Belt/NGS Collection; pages 26–27: © Joel Sartore/NGS Image Collection; pages 28–29: © James L. Amos/Corbis; pages 30–31: AP/World Wide Press

Library of Congress Cataloging-in-Publication Data is available.
ISBN 1-58717-137-6 (reinforced trade edition)
1 3 5 7 9 RTE 10 8 6 4 2
ISBN 1-58717-138-4 (paperback edition)
1 3 5 7 9 PB 10 8 6 4 2
PRINTED IN SINGAPORE BY TIEN WAH PRESS
For more information about our books, and the authors and artists who create them, visit our web site: www.northsouth.com

The air around us is always
moving and changing.
We call these changes weather.

Storms are sudden, violent changes in the weather.

Every second, hundreds
of thunderstorms are born
around the world.
Thunderstorms are
heavy rain showers.
They can drop millions of gallons
of water in just one minute.

During a thunderstorm,
lightning bolts can shoot
between clouds and the ground.
A bolt of lightning
is 50,000 degrees.
That's five times hotter
than the surface of the sun.
Lightning can destroy a tree
or a small house.
It can also start fires
in forests and grasslands.

Thunder is the sound
lightning makes as it
suddenly heats the air.
You can tell how far away
lightning is.
Count the seconds
between the flash of light
and the sound of thunder.
Five seconds equal one mile.

Hailstones are chunks of ice that are tossed up and down by the winds of some thunderstorms. Hail can be the size of a marble or larger than a baseball.

Nearly 5,000 hailstorms strike the United States every year. They can destroy crops and damage buildings and cars.

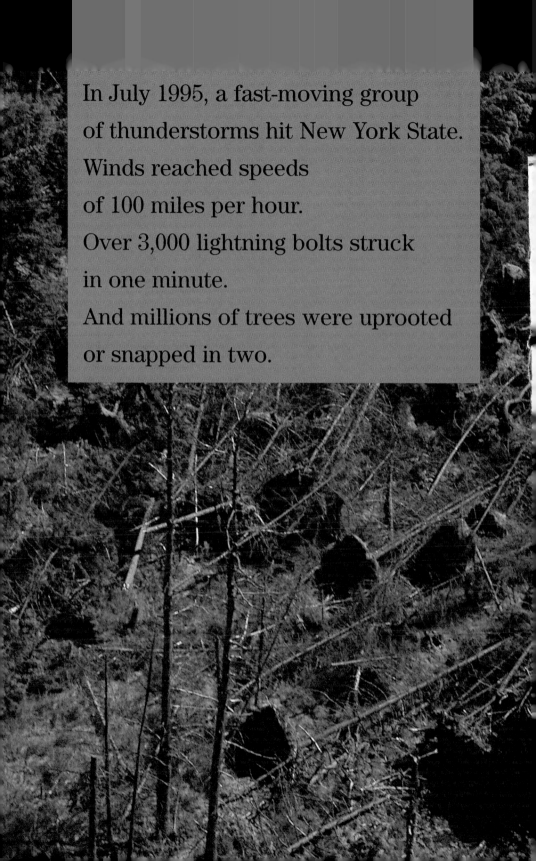

In July 1995, a fast-moving group
of thunderstorms hit New York State.
Winds reached speeds
of 100 miles per hour.
Over 3,000 lightning bolts struck
in one minute.
And millions of trees were uprooted
or snapped in two.

Thunderstorms sometimes give birth to tornadoes. Inside a storm, a funnel-shaped cloud reaches downward. Winds inside a tornado can spin faster than 300 miles per hour. These winds can lift cars off the ground and rip houses apart.

More than 1,000 tornadoes strike
the United States each year.
Most of them form
during spring and summer.
In April 1974, nearly 150
tornadoes struck 13 states
east of the Mississippi River.
More than 300 people were killed
and 5,000 were injured.
Nearly 10,000 homes
were destroyed.

Television and radio stations
often give early alerts.
A tornado **watch** means
that one may strike
during the next few hours.

Number of Tornadoes in the United States

Less than 1 every 2 years

1 to 2 a year

3 to 4 a year

5 to 6 a year

More than 6 a year

A **warning** means a tornado
has been seen by people
or on radar.
During a tornado warning
you should find shelter
in a basement or closet.

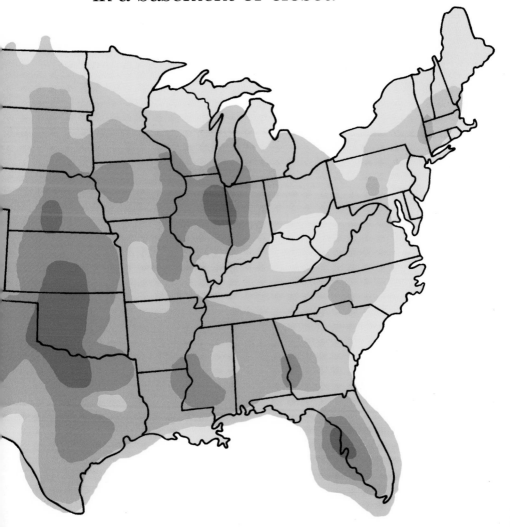

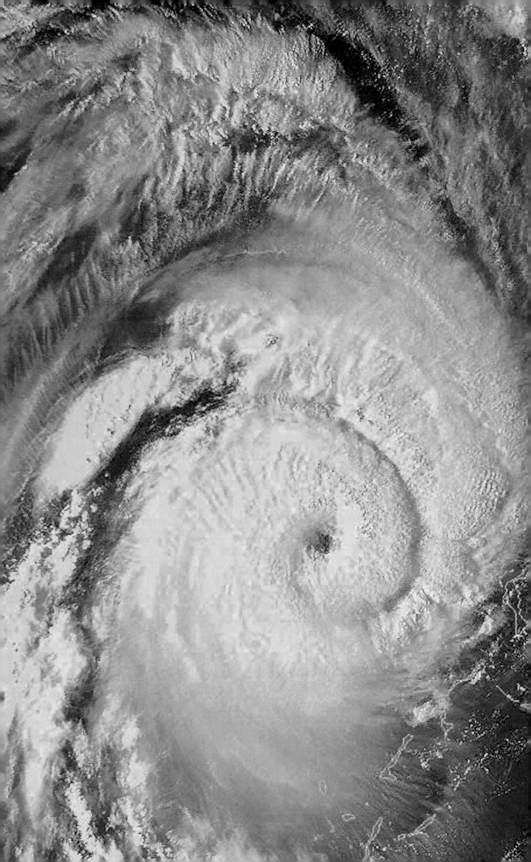

Hurricanes are the deadliest
storms in the world.
They kill more people than
all other storms combined.
Hurricanes stretch for
hundreds of miles.
They have winds of between
74 and 200 miles per hour.
The eye of a hurricane is
the quiet center of the storm.
Inside the eye, the wind
stops blowing, the sun shines,
and the sky is blue.
But beware, the storm
is not over yet.

Hurricanes are born over warm ocean waters from early summer to mid-fall.

When they finally reach land, their pounding waves wash away beaches, boats, and houses.

Their howling winds bend and uproot trees and telephone poles. Their heavy rains cause floods.

In August 1992, Hurricane
Andrew smashed into Florida
and Louisiana.
Over 200,000 people
were left homeless.
In the Pacific Ocean, hurricanes
are called typhoons.
In April 1991, a typhoon hit
the country of Bangladesh.
Over a million homes
were damaged or destroyed.
More than 130,000 people died.

Blizzards are huge snowstorms.
They have winds of at least
35 miles per hour.
Usually at least two inches of snow
falls per hour.
Temperatures are at 20 degrees
or lower.
Falling and blowing snow make
it hard to see in a blizzard.

In March 1993, a major blizzard struck the entire East Coast. Cold temperatures, high winds, and heavy snows hit from Florida to Canada.

Millions of people lost power and spent days in dark, cold homes. Thousands were stuck on snowy highways and in airports when planes were grounded.

No one can prevent storms.
But weather reports can predict
and warn us when a storm
may hit.
The more prepared we are,
the safer we will be
when the next one strikes.